Grace for the Caregiver, Volume II

A 45-Day Christian Devotional for Peace, Hope, and Renewal

Dwane J. Brown

Grace-Filled Press

Published by Grace-Filled Press

Contents

Dedication

To my dearest friend, Steve Stricklin, who, after almost thirty years in San Antonio, sold his home and moved nine hundred miles to care for his elderly mother and uncle. His faithful love and bold obedience show what it truly means to honor God and family.

To Ginny Stricklin, who cared sacrificially for her own mother in her final years and, with the same quiet obedience, moved with Steve to serve their family once more.

To my friend, Hal Hornburg, whose steady care for his wife, Cynthia, was a living sermon of grace and devotion. His life showed me that loving service to a spouse is one of the highest forms of ministry.

To my sister-in-law of more than thirty-five years, Rhonda Hagen, who faithfully cares for her and my wife's parents while working full time and managing her own home. Her steadfast love and strength fill the gap my wife and I cannot, and I thank God for her daily.

To every caregiver walking this sacred road, you are seen, valued, and loved. May you find strength for each day and grace for every moment.

Foreword

Grace. Care. Giving.

These three words that typify my good friend, Dwane Brown. He has not only written about them: he has walked them. I have known Dwane for more than twenty years. In that time, he has grown from a young man carrying a burden for his loved one who was struggling with pain into a man of faith, bearing that same burden, yet now yoked to the One Man who truly carries the weight. Dwane and I have shared our lives together over these many years. In the first part of our life, Dwane looked to me as his pastor and counselor. During that time, we became more than mentor and mentee. He indeed became my best friend. He's been there for me in times of pain and times of joy. He spent years urging me to attend the Walk to Emmaus and I persistently resisted until I could no longer come

3

up with an excuse. The Walk to Emmaus changed my life. I shudder to think what might have been had Dwane not dared to gently intervene in my painful trajectory. His humility and trust in God's grace has changed my life Dwane has learned in these many years about giving care to others through the grace of God. I have experienced his care myself, and yet it seems to me he never even broke a sweat. He must have been empowered by a strength that can only come from above. And this truth and strength he will share with you in these pages.

"And my God will meet all your needs according to thee riches of his glory in Christ Jesus." -Philippians 4:19 NIV

George Fike, Pastor (Retired) CityChurch • San Antonio, TX

Acknowledgments

I AM GRATEFUL TO the pastors, staff, and volunteers of City Church in San Antonio for your ministry and encouragement.

To the Boerne Emmaus Community and the Love Wins Breakfast Club small group, thank you for your fellowship and for the reminders of God's grace that have marked my journey.

To my ministry brothers of more than twenty years, Pastor George Fike and Pastor Mike Meadows, your friendship and partnership in ministry have been a source of strength.

To the Somerset Methodist Church, where I formed the foundation of my faith, I am forever indebted.

To Felix Gonzalez with Boston Media and Design, LLC, for your mentorship and assistance with design, format, distribution, and, most importantly, your love as a brother in Christ.

Finally, I want to express my deep appreciation for the support of my wife, sons, their wives, and my grandchildren.

Introduction

MY NAME IS DWANE Brown, and like many of you, I continue to walk the daily path of caregiving. My wife remains the love of my life and my first ministry. Some days still bring the same mix of work, home responsibilities, and doctor visits, along with the emotions that come from caring for someone you love. Through it all, I keep learning that caregiving isn't just a role, it's a daily invitation to depend on God's grace.

This second volume continues where the first left off, offering new reflections drawn from the same well of faith and experience. The lessons haven't changed much—only deepened. Each day still calls for patience, love, and the quiet courage to keep showing up.

My hope is that over these next 45 days, you'll again find encouragement, perspective, and peace for the road ahead. Whether you've been caring for years or have only recently stepped into this calling, may these readings remind you that you are not alone. There is grace enough for every day, and God walks beside you in them all.

How to Use This Devotional

THIS SECOND VOLUME OF *GRACE for the Caregiver* continues the same simple rhythm of Scripture, reflection, questions, and prayer. It offers forty-five more days of encouragement for your caregiving journey. Whether you are returning from the first book or starting here, may these pages help you pause each day and draw strength from God's Word.

Each day follows a clear pattern:

Scripture: A passage from God's Word to anchor your heart.

Reflection: A short meditation applying God's truth to caregiving.

Questions: Space to reflect or journal if you choose.

Prayer: A closing prayer to surrender the day to God.

The devotional is organized into weekly themes that build on the heart of Volume I, moving from foundations of grace toward deeper trust and renewal:□

Week 1: Love Without Conditions

Week 2: Strength in the Waiting

Week 3: Hope in the Ordinary

Week 4: The Ministry of Presence

Week 5: Faith for the Hard Days

Week 6: Rest for the Weary

Week 7: Living from Overflow

Each week ends with a brief page for reflection and prayer, giving you space to look back and prepare for what lies ahead.

Use this devotional in whatever way serves you best. Read daily, linger on a theme, or return to passages that speak to your heart. Most of all, let these pages remind you that caregiving is not a race but a shared journey. Come not for perfection but for presence, the presence of the God who gives grace for today, peace for the journey, and joy for the soul.

Prayer for the Journey

HEAVENLY FATHER, THANK YOU for walking with me through this journey of caregiving. You have carried me through long nights and uncertain days, and You've taught me that Your grace is new every morning.

As I step into this next season, give me a heart that listens for Your voice in both the stillness and the strain. Strengthen me when the path feels unending. Remind me that Your presence is steady, even when my hands tremble and my faith feels thin.

Teach me to serve with gentleness and hope, to see Your image in the one I care for, and to rest in the assurance that You are working even when I cannot see it.

Let these pages draw me closer to You, Lord. Renew my spirit, deepen my trust, and let every act of care reflect Your love.

In Jesus' name, Amen.

Week 1: Love Without Conditions

Love Without Conditions

DAY 1: PRESENCE OVER PERFECTION

Scripture:

"BE COMPLETELY HUMBLE AND gentle; be patient, bearing with one another in love." – Ephesians 4:2 (NIV)

Devotional Reflection:

Caregiving rarely unfolds the way we imagine. Tasks take longer, tempers shorten, and patience stretches thin. Yet God's invitation is not to perform perfectly but to be present. Love without conditions shows up even when things do not go as planned. It means choosing gentleness instead of control, compassion instead of irritation. Grace does not wait for you to get it right; it meets you right where you are. When you stop striving for perfection, space opens for peace. You begin to see God's fingerprints in the interruptions, in the quiet moments when love simply endures.

Jesus modeled this kind of love throughout His ministry. He never rushed past people in pain but stopped to listen, love, and heal. His love was not transactional but relational. That same love calls you to slow down and see the person, not just the problem. In caregiving, every interruption becomes an invitation to embody His heart. Presence does not promise ease, but it guarantees meaning. When you show up with grace instead of frustration, you reflect the patience of Christ. Each humble act, no matter how small, becomes a declaration that His love is stronger than your exhaustion.

Reflective Questions:

What situations tempt you to focus on performance instead of presence?

Where do you sense God inviting you to slow down and simply be with your loved one?

How might you show patience to yourself as well as to others?

Prayer:

Lord, help me to trade perfection for presence and striving for peace. Teach me that love is not measured by flawless effort but by faithful compassion that shows up even when I feel weary. When impatience rises, remind me how patient You are with me. Fill my heart with gentleness and humility that reflect Yours. Let every act of care become an offering of grace. Amen.

Love Without Conditions

Day 2: The Cost of Compassion

Scripture:

"Carry each other's burdens, and in this way you will fulfill the law of Christ." – Galatians 6:2 (NIV)

Devotional Reflection:

Real love carries weight. Compassion is beautiful, but let's be honest, it is not painless. There are days when empathy feels like exhaustion and serving feels like real sacrifice. The world often celebrates compassion as soft or sentimental, yet Scripture calls it courageous. To carry another's burden means allowing your own shoulders to ache under its weight. This is not weakness; it is divine imitation. Christ bore our pain so that we could learn to bear one another's. Love without conditions costs something, but it also transforms. Each burden carried becomes a quiet sermon of grace.

In John 13, Jesus washed His disciples' feet, the act of a servanthood. He knew betrayal was near, yet He knelt in humility and washed Judas' feet. Compassion does not wait for ideal circumstances; it acts in love despite them. When you serve with a tired body or a weary heart, you are walking in the footsteps of Christ, who loved through fatigue and pain. Compassion that costs you something teaches you to depend on the One who gave everything. When caregiving feels heavy, remember this: love that imitates Christ never goes unseen. God counts every quiet sacrifice, and in His Kingdom, nothing poured out in love is every wasted.

Reflective Questions:

What burdens have you carried that drew you closer to God?

When compassion feels costly, how can you find renewal in Christ's example?

What small act of love might you offer today without expecting recognition?

Prayer:

Jesus, You carried the weight of the world in love and never turned away from those in need. Teach me to carry others' burdens with humility, grace, and quiet strength. When compassion feels heavy, renew my endurance through Your Spirit. Let my love mirror Your steadfast heart, and remind me that every act of service echoes Your own. Amen.

Love Without Conditions

DAY 3: GENTLE STRENGTH

Scripture:

"LET YOUR GENTLENESS BE evident to all. The Lord is near." – Philippians 4:5 (NIV)

Devotional Reflection:

Gentleness is not weakness; it is strength under control. In caregiving, strength often looks loud and busy, but the gentlest moments are often the most powerful. God's strength shows up in a calm word, a steady hand, or a refusal to let frustration rule the heart. The Lord's nearness makes gentleness possible even when everything around you feels tense or rushed. Every time you respond with patience instead of panic, you mirror Christ's heart. This is love without conditions, not powered by circumstance, but anchored in divine peace.

When Jesus encountered the woman caught in adultery, He did not respond with condemnation but with compassion. His gentleness disarmed shame and restored dignity. That same Spirit lives in you, empowering you to respond softly even when circumstances shout for control. Strength is not proven by volume; it is measured by peace under pressure. Gentleness invites the presence of God into ordinary interactions. It does not mean you suppress emotion; it means you choose love over reaction. When your hands tremble and your patience wears thin, remember this: the Lord is near.

Reflective Questions:

Where in your caregiving do you need God's gentle strength right now?

When has gentleness opened a door that anger would have closed?

How can your calm presence minister to someone today?

Prayer:

Father, thank You for being near and steady when my own strength wavers. Fill me with quiet courage and peace that flow from Your Spirit. Let gentleness shape my words and actions so that my care becomes an echo of Your grace. Remind me that strength in You is never harsh or hurried but calm, kind, and full of love. Amen.

Love Without Conditions

DAY 4: SERVING IN SILENCE

Scripture:

"BUT WHEN YOU GIVE to the needy, do not let your left hand know what your right hand is doing." – Matthew 6:3 (NIV)

Devotional Reflection:

Some of the holiest moments in caregiving happen when no one is watching. There are no thank-you cards, no applause, and quite frankly, often no acknowledgment at all. But there is good news! God sees what others overlook. Silence does not mean insignificance. Quite the contrary. In the quiet corners of daily service, His love flows through you, unseen yet unmistakably present. Every unseen act of kindness writes a story of grace that heaven records with joy. Serving in silence purifies motive and it draws the focus away from reward and back to love itself.

Jesus Himself lived a life marked by quiet service. Before His miracles, before His public ministry, He spent upwards of 30 years in obscurity working, listening, praying, and waiting. When you serve without recognition, you are walking His same humble path. Love without conditions does not need applause to have purpose. The smallest act, done in faith, carries eternal weight. When the world forgets your effort, remember that God never does.

Reflective Questions:

When have you felt unseen in your caregiving?

How can serving quietly draw you closer to God's heart?

What truth can remind you that your work matters even when it goes unnoticed?

Prayer:

Father, thank You for seeing what others overlook and for finding beauty in the quiet acts no one else notices. When I feel invisible, remind me that You are near, watching with love and delight. Teach me to serve without seeking credit, to love without counting the cost, and to rest in the truth that Your approval is enough. Shape my heart to mirror Yours, gentle and faithful in every hidden moment. Let each small act of care become an offering of worship to You. Amen.

Love Without Conditions

Day 5: Compassion Fatigue

Scripture:

"Come to me, all you who are weary and burdened, and I will give you rest." – Matthew 11:28 (NIV)

Devotional Reflection:

Compassion is beautiful, but it can also be draining. When you continually pour yourself out for others, the weight of care can start to feel too heavy. Even love has limits when carried in human strength alone. Compassion fatigue is not a failure of faith; it is a sign that you have been giving deeply. Jesus invites you to bring your weariness to Him, not to hide it or feel ashamed of it. True rest is not found in escape but in renewal through His presence. He knows every tear, every sigh, every sacrifice.

Resting in Christ does not mean abandoning your calling. It means letting Him sustain it. When you pause in His presence, you remember that you were never meant to do this alone. His Spirit replenishes what compassion has drained. The same Jesus who healed multitudes also withdrew to quiet places to pray. If even the Savior of the World needed rest, guess what? So do you. Let your fatigue drive you toward His peace, not away from it.

Reflective Questions:

What signs show that your compassion is running low?

How can you intentionally rest in God this week?

What helps you remember that caregiving is a shared work with Christ?

Prayer:

Lord, You see the places where my strength runs thin and my spirit feels worn. I have poured out in love, and now I come to You empty-handed, trusting that You are enough. Quiet my striving and breathe Your peace into my exhaustion. Teach me to rest, not out of weakness, but out of faith that You are working even as I pause. Restore my joy, renew my compassion, and let Your presence be the well that never runs dry. Amen.

Love Without Conditions

DAY 6: RECEIVING LOVE

Scripture:

"WE LOVE BECAUSE HE first loved us." – 1 John 4:19 (NIV)

Devotional Reflection:

Many caregivers find it easier to give love than to receive it. You are quick to meet others' needs but hesitant to let anyone meet yours. Yet God designed love to flow both ways, received and given. When you resist being loved, you quietly tell yourself that grace is for others but not for you. You often refuse to ask for help. Receiving love is not selfish, it is sacred. It restores balance and reminds you that you are also God's beloved child, not merely His servant.

Jesus received love freely from the Father in prayer, from friends who served Him, from Mary who poured perfume on His feet. He did not reject care, for self or others, as weakness. He showed that humility includes allowing others to bless you. The same grace that empowers you to love also calls you to receive. Let others hold you up when your strength falters. Love without conditions is not one-directional, it is a holy exchange of giving and receiving that keeps the heart whole.

Reflective Questions:

Why is it sometimes difficult for you to receive love or help?

What might change if you accepted care and help from others as part of grace?

How has God shown His love for you through others recently?

Prayer:

Father, melt the pride that makes me strong on the outside but weary within. Teach me to open my hands, to receive love, help, and care without apology or fear. Let me feel Your tenderness in the kindness of others, and remind me that I am not beyond the reach of grace. Where I have built walls around my heart, break them gently with Your mercy. Fill me until I overflow again with the love that begins and ends in You. Amen.

Love Without Conditions

DAY 7: GRATITUDE PRACTICE

Scripture:

"GIVE THANKS TO THE Lord, for he is good; his love endures forever." – Psalm 107:1 (NIV)

Devotional Reflection:

Gratitude is the rhythm that keeps love alive. It's the steady beat beneath the noise of each day, the quiet drum that holds your heart in time with God's grace. It shifts your focus from what is missing to what God is doing. When days blur together and weariness sets in, gratitude becomes the bridge between exhaustion and joy. Giving thanks is not denial of hardship. It is acknowledgment that grace exists even within it. Each moment of gratitude re-centers your heart on God's goodness, not your circumstances. It teaches you to see beauty where others see burden, blessing where others see duty.

Love without conditions flourishes when gratitude takes root. The more you thank God for His daily mercies, the more aware you become of His presence in every task. Gratitude does not change the work, but it changes you in the work. It softens frustration and opens space for peace. Even in chaos, you can whisper, "Thank You, Lord," and find your heart kept in rhythm by His faithfulness.

Reflective Questions:

When your days feel off-beat or chaotic, what helps you return to God's rhythm of grace?

How does gratitude steady your heart when life's tempo feels too fast?

Where do you sense God inviting you to pause, listen, and find His rhythm again today?

Prayer:

Father, thank You for keeping my heart in rhythm when the world feels out of tune. Teach me to listen for Your steady beat of grace beneath the noise of my days. When I rush ahead or lose tempo in my spirit, draw me back to the pulse of Your peace. Let gratitude rise in me like a quiet drum that steadies my thoughts and softens my heart. Keep my spirit in time with

Yours so that even in weariness, I move with joy and rest in Your unshakable love. Amen.

Love Without Conditions

WEEKLY NOTES AND PRAYERS

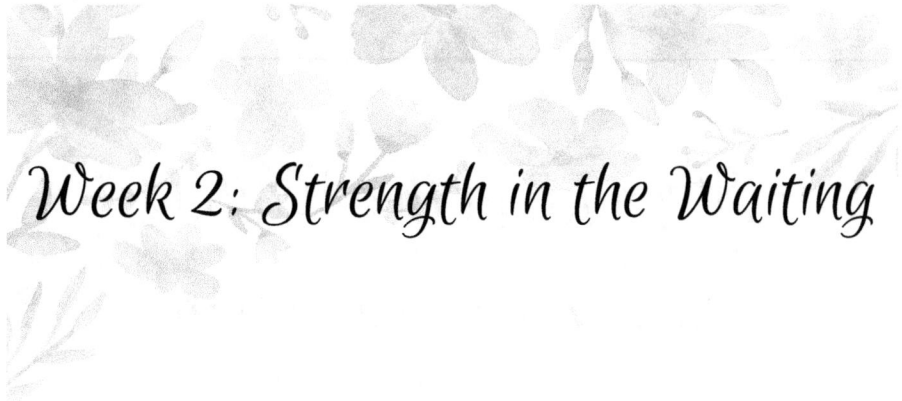

Week 2: Strength in the Waiting

Strength in the Waiting

Day 1: When God Seems Silent

Scripture:

"THE LORD WILL FIGHT for you; you need only to be still." – Exodus 14:14 (NIV)

Devotional Reflection:

There are moments in caregiving when the silence of God feels louder than any prayer you have ever prayed. You cry out for relief or direction, yet heaven seems quiet. In those moments, doubt whispers that perhaps God has stepped away, that maybe your situation is too big, too small, or too repetitive to matter to Him. But silence is not abandonment. It is often the sacred pause where your trust in Him is tested and deepened. The God who spoke creation into being has not forgotten how to speak, He simply knows that sometimes His stillness accomplishes more than His speech.

In the waiting, your faith grows deeper roots. Stillness becomes an act of worship when you choose to believe that God is working even when you cannot see it. The Israelites stood before the Red Sea, surrounded by fear and uncertainty, but the Lord was preparing a miracle that only silence alone could hold. When your prayers echo without reply, hold fast to the truth that God's quiet is not His absence, it is the soil where trust takes root. Waiting in silence may be the holiest form of listening.

Reflective Questions:

Where have you experienced God's silence in your caregiving journey?

How can you use silence as an opportunity to trust more deeply?

What might God be shaping in your faith during quiet seasons?

Prayer:

Lord, when You seem silent, help me trust that Your hand is still moving even when I cannot see it. Calm my fears and quiet my restless heart so I can rest in Your presence. Teach me to wait with confidence, believing that stillness is not absence but preparation. Strengthen my faith to hold steady until Your timing unfolds in peace. Amen.

Strength in the Waiting

Day 2: Trusting Delay

Scripture:

"For the revelation awaits an appointed time; though it linger, wait for it; it will certainly come and will not delay." – Habakkuk 2:3 (NIV)

Devotional Reflection:

Waiting can feel like wasted time, but in God's hands, delay becomes discipline. Caregivers live with constant tension between what they hope for and what they can handle. It is tempting to assume that if God truly cared, He would hurry. Yet faith learns to rest not in speed, but in sovereignty. His delays are not denials. They are invitations to lean harder on grace. In the pauses, God is shaping your strength and deepening your trust. The unseen work beneath the surface often matters more than the visible results. Waiting is not the absence of God's movement but the space where

His purpose matures. When you cannot see progress, remember that He is never still.

When you trust God's timing, you declare that His wisdom outruns your impatience. Each delay shapes you for His purposes. Waiting refines love, stretches faith, and teaches surrender. It loosens your grip on control and reminds you that peace comes from presence, not progress. God's pace is not punishment, it is protection. He sees the whole picture, from beginning to end, and knows exactly what must grow in you before His plan unfolds around you. What feels like delay may be divine timing, preparing you for blessings that require the strength only waiting can build. Every moment of waiting is an opportunity to rest in His care, to be held steady by His grace, and to trust that what He begins, He will finish in perfect time.

Reflective Questions:

What current delay in your life might God be using to grow your faith?

How can you shift from frustration to trust during seasons of waiting?

Who in Scripture models patience that encourages you today?

Prayer:

Father, help me to trust Your perfect timing even when my heart longs for quick answers. Teach me to see Your purpose in every pause and to find peace in the waiting. When I grow restless, remind me that faith flourishes in stillness and that waiting with You is never wasted time. Strengthen my heart to rest in Your wisdom and move only at Your pace. Amen.

Strength in the Waiting

Day 3: Holy Frustration

Scripture:

"My grace is sufficient for you, for my power is made perfect in weakness." – 2 Corinthians 12:9 (NIV)

Devotional Reflection:

Frustration often feels like failure, but in God's hands, it becomes formation. When progress slows or prayers seem unanswered, grace is quietly at work beneath the surface. Paul's thorn remained, yet he discovered that divine strength shines brightest through human frailty. Your limitations do not block God's plan, they reveal His presence. Holy frustration is not the absence of faith but an invitation to deeper surrender.

When caregiving feels like one step forward and two steps back, frustration can either harden the heart or humble it. God uses that tension to refine trust, shifting your focus from what you cannot control to what He continues to sustain. Every sigh, every weary prayer, every unmet expectation can become sacred space when you bring it honestly before Him. Growth often begins where your ability ends. Let grace turn irritation into insight and impatience into intercession. The next time you feel stuck, remember that God is still shaping something unseen. His grace doesn't always remove the struggle, but it always redeems it.

Reflective Questions:

Where are you frustrated in your caregiving journey today?

How might God be using this frustration to teach dependence?

What changes when you invite grace into your disappointment?

Prayer:

Father, meet me in my frustration and remind me that You are still at work when I cannot see it. Turn my impatience into prayer and my weakness into worship. Teach me to find purpose in every pause and peace in every delay. Let Your strength fill the space where mine ends and renew my heart with grace. Amen.

Strength in the Waiting

DAY 4: SURRENDERED CONTROL

Scripture:

"TRUST IN THE LORD with all your heart and lean not on your own understanding." – Proverbs 3:5 (NIV)

Devotional Reflection:

Caregiving often demands structure, routine, and planning, but control can quietly become a false comfort. You can organize your day, but you cannot manage outcomes. True peace begins when you release the illusion that you have to hold everything together. Surrender is not weakness; it is trust in motion. When you hand God the reins, the weight of responsibility shifts from your shoulders to His. Peace replaces pressure because you no longer have to be the one holding it all.

Jesus modeled this surrender in the garden when He prayed, "Not My will, but Yours be done." Even in anguish, He trusted the Father's wisdom over His own understanding. Faith does not demand clarity; it yields to divine direction. Each moment you choose trust over control, you make room for grace to work in ways your effort never could. God's hands are steadier than yours, His plans wiser, His timing perfect. What you release, He redeems. Every surrendered plan becomes a stage for His faithfulness to be seen. Trust does not shrink your role, it sanctifies it.

Reflective Questions:

What do you struggle most to release to God's control?

How does surrender bring peace to your daily routine?

What would trusting God fully look like this week?

Prayer:

Lord, I surrender what I cannot control and place it fully in Your hands. Replace my worry with trust and my striving with rest. Teach me to yield my plans and follow Your wisdom with a peaceful heart. Remind me that surrender is strength, not defeat, and that Your will always leads to grace. Amen.

Strength in the Waiting

Day 5: Patience as Faith

Scripture:

"We do not want you to become lazy, but to imitate those who through faith and patience inherit what has been promised." – Hebrews 6:12 (NIV)

Devotional Reflection:

Patience is not passive. It is active trust stretched over time. It is faith that chooses to keep believing when sight gives no reason to. In caregiving, where progress is often slow and outcomes uncertain, patience becomes a daily act of worship. Every long night, every prayer waiting for an answer, becomes a quiet declaration that God is still faithful. His timing may not satisfy your urgency, but it always serves His purpose.

Those who wait well are those who believe well. Patience is not the absence of motion, it is the presence of peace in motion. It keeps you anchored when emotions pull and exhaustion tempts you to quit. The saints before you endured with grace because they knew delay does not mean denial. Abraham waited for a son, Joseph for deliverance, and Hannah for her prayer to be answered. They discovered that waiting with faith is not wasted, it is rewarded. When you learn to wait well, you reflect the steady heart of God Himself. Each act of patience declares that His promise is worth the wait and His presence is enough for today.

Reflective Questions:

Where is God asking you to be patient right now?

How does patience reflect your trust in His promises?

What can you learn from others who waited faithfully?

Prayer:

Father, teach me to see patience as faith that breathes in rhythm with Your will. Strengthen me when waiting feels long and uncertain. Help me to rest in Your promises, trusting that Your timing is perfect. Let endurance grow deep roots in my heart and produce peace that outlasts every delay. Amen.

Strength in the Waiting

DAY 6: WHEN GOD FEELS SILENT

Scripture:

"BE STILL BEFORE THE Lord and wait patiently for Him." – Psalm 37:7 (NIV)

Devotional Reflection:

Silence from God does not mean He has withdrawn. It may mean He is drawing you closer. When the noise quiets and prayers seem to echo unanswered, God is often doing His most delicate work beneath the surface. Stillness becomes sacred space where faith matures and dependence deepens. Feelings fade, but trust is refined. When you stop straining for explanation and rest instead in expectation, you begin to sense His quiet presence.

God works gently in the soil of waiting. What feels like distance may actually be invitation to listen, to slow, to notice His hand in the smallest details. His silence is never absence. It is the pause between promise and fulfillment. Every moment of stillness trains your heart to lean on His character rather than your certainty. Even when you cannot hear His voice, His Word still speaks, and His Spirit still sustains. Faith that endures silence learns to rest, not in answers, but in assurance. Trust grows deepest when the world is quiet and your soul chooses to believe that God is still near.

Reflective Questions:

When have you struggled to sense God's presence?

How can stillness deepen your faith rather than weaken it?

What truth about God anchors you when you feel alone?

Prayer:

Lord, teach me to find You in the silence and not fear the quiet. Calm my restless thoughts and steady my breathing until peace returns. When You seem far away, remind me that You are still near. Help me rest in the truth that Your faithfulness never fades, even when Your voice is still. Strengthen my heart to trust Your unseen work. Amen.

Strength in the Waiting

DAY 7: RENEWAL THROUGH STILLNESS

Scripture:

"IN REPENTANCE AND REST is your salvation, in quietness and trust is your strength." – Isaiah 30:15 (NIV)

Devotional Reflection:

Rest restores what worry steals. When you pause to breathe and listen, you return to God's rhythm. This is a pace set not by urgency, but by grace. Stillness is not idleness, it is intimacy. Renewal happens when you stop striving to do and start learning to be. In stillness, the noise of fear and fatigue begins to fade, and your heart grows sensitive again to God's quiet direction.

True strength flows from surrender. It is not found in effort but in trust, not in endless doing but in holy resting. Stillness resets your spirit and renews your calling. The moments you spend in quiet with God are not wasted. These moments are sacred exchanges where exhaustion turns into peace and purpose is rekindled. Each time you step back from the noise, you make space for His Spirit to breathe new life into yours. The more you rest in Him, the more clearly His calm radiates through you. Renewal is not a reward for hard work. It is a gift for those willing to be still and let God restore what striving has drained.

Reflective Questions:

What does true spiritual rest look like for you?

How can you build stillness into your daily routine?

Where do you sense God inviting you to slow down and renew your strength?

Prayer:

Father, thank You for the gift of stillness that refreshes my soul. Teach me to rest in You without guilt, fear, anxiety, or hurry. Quiet the noise within me so I can hear Your voice clearly again. Restore my heart, renew my purpose, and let Your peace flow through my life. Help me to live from rest, not rush, trusting Your steady rhythm of grace. Amen.

Strength in the Waiting

WEEKLY NOTES AND PRAYERS

Week 3: Hope in the Ordinary

Hope in the Ordinary

DAY 1: DISHES AS WORSHIP

Scripture:

"WHATEVER YOU DO, WORK at it with all your heart, as working for the Lord, not for human masters." – Colossians 3:23 (NIV)

Devotional Reflection:

Caregiving is filled with repetitive, often monotonous routines that test your patience and resolve. The dishes pile up, laundry waits, dust gathers in the curio cabinet, and the quiet moments stretch long. These small acts rarely feel spiritual, yet God meets you in them. Every task done in love carries eternal weight and unseen glory. The kitchen sink becomes an altar when your heart turns toward Him. The ordinary rhythms of life, infused with faith and gentleness, reveal the beauty of grace in motion. Worship does not require a platform or song; it begins wherever humility stoops to serve, even when no one else notices.

Jesus transformed the simple into sacred. When He washed His disciples' feet, He proved that no act of service is too small to hold divine meaning. When you scrub a dish or fold a blanket, you are practicing love in its truest form: selfless, unseen, and steadfast. God's presence sanctifies every gesture done in faith. What you call mundane, heaven calls holy. The goal is not to finish faster, but to serve deeper and love longer, knowing that each quiet offering echoes eternity.

Reflective Questions:

What task today feels too small to matter?

How could you treat your daily chores as moments of worship?

Where might gratitude shift how you see the ordinary?

Prayer:

Lord, meet me in my daily tasks. Let the work of my hands reflect Your love and my routines become praise to You. Teach me to serve with joy and patience, even when no one else sees it. Remind me daily that every act of care is sacred when offered to You, and let my heart rest in that truth. Amen.

Hope in the Ordinary

Day 2: Sacred Small Talk

Scripture:

"Let your conversation be always full of grace, seasoned with salt, so that you may know how to answer everyone." – Colossians 4:6 (NIV)

Devotional Reflection:

Caregiving often revolves around practical questions: doctor updates, meals, medications, schedules. Yet within those small exchanges lies sacred potential. The kindness in your tone, the patience in your pause, and the smile you share may be the only sermon someone hears today. God uses small talk to build big connections and to whisper His love into weary hearts. When you listen with compassion, you offer healing no medicine can match. Grace begins not in grand speeches but in everyday words spoken with care and sincerity.

Jesus transformed ordinary conversations into moments of redemption. He talked with fishermen, tax collectors, and strangers who had lost hope, and each exchange revealed the Father's heart. You carry that same Spirit into every conversation. When your words bring gentleness, patience, and peace, you reflect His love. Speaking slowly, listening deeply, and responding kindly are not small things, they are sacred practices that open space for grace to move. The holy often hides in small talk when the heart is open.

Reflective Questions:

Who might need a gentle word from you today?

When was the last time you listened without rushing?

How can you turn ordinary talk into a moment of grace?

Prayer:

Father, guide my words and soften my tone. Let my conversations carry kindness and truth. Use my voice to lift others and remind them of Your love. Help me see every exchange as a chance to serve. Amen.

Hope in the Ordinary

DAY 3: EVERYDAY MIRACLES

Scripture:

"THE LORD HAS DONE great things for us, and we are filled with joy." – Psalm 126:3 (NIV)

Devotional Reflection:

Some miracles arrive without fanfare. They show up quietly: in a breath of calm after chaos, in laughter breaking tension, in the strength that surprises you when you thought you had none left. Caregiving is filled with these small mercies that go unnoticed unless you pause to look. The world expects miracles to be spectacular, but faith teaches that the extraordinary often hides in plain sight. Gratitude tunes your heart to notice God's work where others see routine. When you begin to thank Him in the middle of the mess, you start to see His fingerprints on everything. Even the smallest grace becomes proof that heaven still reaches earth.

Jesus gave thanks before multiplying bread and fish. His gratitude turned scarcity into abundance. When you thank God for what you already have, you open space for joy to grow. Each breath, each shared moment, is a reminder that grace is active and present. Miracles happen when faith sees through the ordinary. What changes is not the world around you but your awareness of God within it.

Reflective Questions:

What small mercy did you experience today?

How has gratitude opened your eyes to God's presence?

Where might a miracle already be unfolding in your care?

Prayer:

Lord, open my eyes to Your wonders in the ordinary. Help me celebrate small mercies and recognize the quiet miracles You place in each day. Let gratitude shape my vision so that joy becomes my natural response, even in moments that feel routine or unseen. Amen.

Hope in the Ordinary

DAY 4: HUMOR AS HEALING

Scripture:

"A CHEERFUL HEART IS good medicine, but a crushed spirit dries up the bones." – Proverbs 17:22 (NIV)

Devotional Reflection:

Laughter and faith belong together. Humor cuts through tension and restores balance to weary souls. In caregiving, it becomes a form of holy resistance, a reminder that light still shines in dark places. God created laughter as medicine for the heart. When you share joy, even in hardship, you reclaim hope from despair. A smile does not dismiss pain; it dignifies it by choosing joy in spite of it.

Jesus embodied joy. His presence drew crowds not only because of His miracles but because of His warmth. When you allow yourself to laugh, you are practicing trust, the belief that God's goodness still surrounds you. Humor breaks the weight of perfection and invites humanity back into the moment. Each laugh shared with your loved one becomes an act of healing, a spark of resurrection in the middle of fatigue.

Reflective Questions:

When did you last allow yourself to laugh freely?

How could humor become part of your healing rhythm?

What does joy look like in your caregiving today?

Prayer:

God of joy, thank You for laughter that lifts the soul. Help me find humor even in hard places. Remind me that every smile is a gift from You. Let joy rise in my heart as a sign of trust in Your goodness. Amen.

Hope in the Ordinary

Day 5: Gratitude Lists

Scripture:

"Give thanks in all circumstances; for this is God's will for you in Christ Jesus." – 1 Thessalonians 5:18 (NIV)

Devotional Reflection:

Gratitude is not denial, it is declaration. Writing down blessings is a simple act that guards the heart from despair. When you make a habit of thanksgiving, you begin to see God's fingerprints everywhere. Gratitude grounds you in reality while keeping your spirit lifted. It is the discipline of remembrance, the practice of noticing how much grace surrounds you. Caregiving becomes lighter when you name what is still good.

Each list of thanks becomes a hymn of hope. When you write out what you are grateful for, you are telling your soul the truth; it is well. God's mercy threads through every day, even the ones that ache. Gratitude transforms exhaustion into perspective and scarcity into abundance. The more you name, the more you see that God has never stopped providing. Thanksgiving is the rhythm of grace made visible.

Reflective Questions:

What three things are you thankful for today?

How does gratitude change your outlook on care?

What is one small blessing you can thank God for right now?

Prayer:

Lord, teach me the language of gratitude. Help me name my blessings and rest in Your goodness. Fill my heart with thanks in every season. Let thanksgiving shape my thoughts until joy becomes second nature. Amen.

Hope in the Ordinary

DAY 6: SEEING THROUGH GOD'S EYES

Scripture:

"THE LORD DOES NOT look at the things people look at. People look at the outward appearance, but the Lord looks at the heart." – 1 Samuel 16:7 (NIV)

Devotional Reflection:

The world judges by appearance, success, beauty, and ability, but God looks at the heart. He sees courage beneath weakness and strength beneath sorrow. In caregiving, it is easy to focus on what is lost, yet God sees what is still being shaped. Every act of compassion reflects His image and reveals His character through you. When you start to see others through His eyes, you begin to notice the divine hidden in the familiar. Love grows deeper when judgment gives way to grace, and mercy becomes your natural response.

Jesus saw potential where others saw brokenness. He restored dignity to those the world ignored and offered hope to those who felt invisible. Seeing through God's eyes means choosing compassion over criticism and tenderness over control. It invites you to slow down and truly see people, not just problems. This vision changes everything; it turns frustration into intercession and fatigue into love. The ordinary becomes radiant when viewed through heaven's lens, reminding you that every moment can reflect His glory.

Reflective Questions:

Where might God be asking you to see with compassion?

Who in your life needs to be seen with new eyes of grace?

How might this change how you serve today?

Prayer:

Lord, give me Your eyes to see others as You do. Help me recognize beauty where the world sees burden and patience where the world sees weakness. Teach me to slow down, listen with love, and notice Your image in every face I meet. Fill my heart with understanding that transforms the way I serve, and let my compassion mirror Your own. Amen.

Hope in the Ordinary

DAY 7: ORDINARY HOLINESS

Scripture:

"Be holy, because I am holy." – 1 Peter 1:16 (NIV)

Devotional Reflection:

Holiness is not about grandeur; it's about grace lived daily. You do not need to chase a spotlight to live a sacred life. God's presence sanctifies ordinary places: your kitchen, your car, your caregiving moments. Each quiet act of love is worship in motion. Holiness happens when you choose faithfulness over frustration and compassion over convenience. The sacred often hides where the world is too busy to look.

Jesus blessed ordinary bread before breaking it, transforming a meal into communion. In the same way, your daily offerings become holy when given in love. God's holiness does not demand perfection; it invites participation. When you walk with Him through routine and repetition, you begin to see that every moment, however small, can carry divine meaning. The holy is not rare; it is simply recognized.

Reflective Questions:

How can you invite God into your daily routines?

What does ordinary holiness look like for you for your upcoming week?

Where might God be calling you to see sacred purpose today?

Prayer:

Lord, make my ordinary life holy. Let my actions reflect Your love and my heart stay open to Your presence. Teach me to find sacred meaning in every moment You give. Let even my smallest deeds bring You glory. Amen.

Hope in the Ordinary

WEEKLY NOTES AND PRAYERS

Week 4: The Ministry of Presence

The Ministry of Presence

DAY 1: LISTENING WELL

Scripture:

"Everyone should be quick to listen, slow to speak and slow to become angry." – James 1:19 (NIV)

Devotional Reflection:

In caregiving, listening is one of the greatest gifts you can offer. True listening goes beyond hearing words; it means attending to the heart behind them. It requires patience, humility, and the willingness to be fully present. In a world that prizes quick fixes and constant talking, slowing down to listen becomes an act of love. You do not have to have the right words; sometimes the holiest thing you can do is to sit quietly and let another person know they are seen and heard.

Jesus listened to people others ignored. He paused for blind beggars, for children, for outcasts, for the broken and the fearful. His listening restored dignity before He ever spoke a word of healing. When you listen well, you reflect that same grace. You create space for God's peace to enter conversations where pain has been bottled up too long. Listening well does not fix problems; it allows the presence of Christ to settle where words would only crowd.

Reflective Questions:

Who needs you to listen without offering advice today?

How can you prepare your heart to listen with patience and grace?

When has someone's listening presence brought healing to you?

Prayer:

Lord, teach me to listen as You listen. Quiet my urge to speak and help me hear with compassion. Let my presence bring comfort where words cannot. Give me patience when I grow weary and grace when silence feels awkward. Fill the quiet moments with Your peace, and let those I serve sense Your love through my attentiveness. May every conversation become a doorway for Your healing presence. Amen.

The Ministry of Presence

DAY 2: THE POWER OF TOUCH

Scripture:

"Jesus reached out his hand and touched the man. 'I am willing,' he said. 'Be clean!'" – Matthew 8:3 (NIV)

Devotional Reflection:

Human beings are wired for connection. From the moment of birth, a gentle embrace can calm fear and steady the heart. The simple act of caring for someone physically—helping them stand, offering a steady hand, or tucking a blanket around their shoulders—can speak love more clearly than words ever could. In caregiving, these moments are sacred. They remind both giver and receiver that presence matters more than perfection. Compassion expressed through touch or gentle care restores a sense of belonging that illness or isolation often steals away.

Jesus' ministry was filled with healing through connection. He reached for the untouchable and restored their dignity before speaking a word. His hands carried grace where others carried judgment. When you serve with tenderness, you continue His ministry in your own quiet way. Your care may not draw crowds or headlines, but heaven notices every act done in love. Through your hands, hearts can heal. Through your presence, peace can return.

Reflective Questions:

When have you felt God's compassion through someone's care?

What small act of kindness can you offer today that reminds another person they are not alone?

How might God use your presence to bring healing in quiet ways?

Prayer:

Jesus, thank You for showing compassion through Your healing touch. Use my hands to bring comfort where there is pain and warmth where there is loneliness. Fill my actions with gentleness and my heart with patience. When words fall short, let my care become a language of grace. Teach me to see every moment of service as a sacred opportunity to reveal Your love. May my presence remind others that they are not forgotten, for You are near. Amen.

The Ministry of Presence

DAY 3: SILENT PRAYER

Scripture:

"Be still, and know that I am God." – Psalm 46:10 (NIV)

Devotional Reflection:

Prayer does not always require words. Sometimes silence is the truest prayer. In caregiving, exhaustion can make it hard to find words for what you feel. Yet God hears the groans of the heart as clearly as spoken sentences. Silent prayer is surrender, it is resting your spirit in God's presence and trusting that He knows your need before you can name it. Sitting quietly before Him is not emptiness; it is full awareness that He is near.

Jesus often withdrew to quiet places to pray. His example shows that silence is not absence of faith but its deep expression. In stillness, you allow your heart to breathe again. You let God speak in the spaces between thoughts. Silent prayer teaches you to rely on His presence rather than your performance. Even five quiet minutes in the middle of chaos can restore your strength and remind you that you are not carrying the weight alone.

Reflective Questions:

When was the last time you sat quietly in God's presence?

How can silence become part of your prayer life this week?

What happens when you stop talking and simply rest before God?

Prayer:

Lord, meet me in the silence and quiet my restless thoughts. When words fail, let Your peace fill the empty spaces. Teach me to rest in Your presence and trust that You are near. Help me listen more deeply than I speak, and find renewal in stillness before You. Amen.

The Ministry of Presence

DAY 4: BEARING ANOTHER'S BURDEN

Scripture:

"CARRY EACH OTHER'S BURDENS, and in this way you will fulfill the law of Christ." – Galatians 6:2 (NIV)

Devotional Reflection:

To bear another's burden is sacred work. It means walking beside someone in their pain without trying to fix it or rush it away. In caregiving, you shoulder the weight of another person's needs, fears, and hopes. This kind of love costs something; it stretches your patience, your time, and your heart. Yet in sharing another's load, you fulfill the very heart of Christ's command. You become a living reflection of His compassion, the same compassion that carried the cross on your behalf. Bearing another's burden reminds the hurting that they are not forgotten, that God's love is present through the hands and hearts of His people.

Jesus bore the burdens of humanity in both body and soul. He understands the exhaustion that comes from loving deeply and serving faithfully. When you carry another's weight with gentleness, you walk in His footsteps and find strength in His grace. Bearing another's burden is not about being strong; it is about drawing strength from the One who never fails. You were never meant to carry alone. When love is shared, it grows lighter, and when Christ stands beside you, even the heaviest load becomes holy ground.

Reflective Questions:

Whose burden are you helping carry right now?

How can you balance empathy with dependence on God?

What does it mean to let Christ carry the weight with you?

Prayer:

Lord, teach me to carry the burdens of others with humility and compassion. Give me strength that flows from Your heart, not my own. When I grow tired, remind me that You carry me as I carry others. Let my presence bring comfort, and my care point people back to You. May every act of service reflect the mercy of Christ who bore it all for me. Amen.

The Ministry of Presence

DAY 5: WORDS THAT HEAL

Scripture:

"GRACIOUS WORDS ARE A honeycomb, sweet to the soul and healing to the bones." – Proverbs 16:24 (NIV)

Devotional Reflection:

Words hold power, the power to wound or to heal. In caregiving, the way you speak can calm a storm or stir one up. Tone, timing, and tenderness all matter. Speaking gently does not mean avoiding truth; it means delivering it with love. When emotions run high, a soft answer can open hearts where harshness would close them. Every conversation becomes a chance to offer grace, to speak life into someone who feels weary or forgotten. Healing words do not erase pain, but they remind the listener that love is still near and that God has not turned away. Your voice can become a vessel of peace when it carries compassion instead of frustration.

Jesus spoke with both truth and tenderness. His words restored dignity to the broken and hope to the fearful. He did not speak to impress but to transform. When He said, "Peace, be still," even the wind and waves obeyed. The same Spirit that guided His words now lives in you. When you pause before speaking and invite the Holy Spirit to guide your response, your words become part of God's healing work. Choose encouragement over complaint, gentleness over haste, mercy over judgment. Each time you speak with grace, you plant seeds of healing that may take root long after the conversation ends.

Reflective Questions:

When have healing words changed your day or perspective?

What helps you pause before speaking during stressful moments?

How might you use your voice to lift someone's spirit today?

Prayer:

Father, make my words gentle and wise. Let my speech reflect the kindness of Christ and bring peace to those who hear it. When I am tempted to speak out of frustration, guard my tongue and guide my heart. Fill my mouth with grace that strengthens and restores. May my words carry hope that reminds others of Your steadfast love. Amen.

The Ministry of Presence

DAY 6: BOUNDARIES AS MERCY

Scripture:

"LET YOUR 'YES' BE yes, and your 'No,' no; anything beyond this comes from the evil one." – Matthew 5:37 (NIV)

Devotional Reflection:

Boundaries are not walls; they are wisdom shaped by love. In caregiving, saying no can feel like failure, yet healthy limits make compassion sustainable. Without them, care easily turns into exhaustion, and service can become resentment. Setting boundaries is not rejection but protection of what is sacred. It allows you to serve from strength rather than depletion. Mercy sometimes looks like rest, space, or quiet moments away from the demands of the day. Boundaries are how you honor God's design for rhythm: rest, giving and receiving, speaking and silence. They remind you

74

that you are human and that only God can meet every need. Jesus modeled boundaries throughout His ministry. He withdrew from crowds, took time to pray, and rested even when people still needed Him. His love was not diminished by His limits; it was deepened through obedience to the Father's rhythm. When you follow His example, you discover that saying no can be a holy act of trust. Love does not require constant doing; it requires faithfulness within your capacity. Setting boundaries is not selfishness but stewardship of grace. It protects the tender heart God has given you so it can keep loving well for the long journey ahead.

Reflective Questions:

Where might God be calling you to set healthy limits?

How do boundaries help love last longer?

What small change could protect your energy and peace this week?

Prayer:

Lord, help me see that boundaries are gifts of mercy, not signs of my weakness. Teach me to rest without guilt and to serve without resentment. Give me courage to say no when my spirit needs renewal. Fill the spaces I surrender with Your peace and presence. Let my limits become places where Your strength begins. Amen.

The Ministry of Presence

DAY 7: PRESENCE AS PRAYER

Scripture:

"THE LORD IS NEAR to all who call on him, to all who call on him in truth." – Psalm 145:18 (NIV)

Devotional Reflection:

Sometimes the best prayer is simply showing up. Presence itself can be holy, a quiet testimony that love remains. When words fail, your steady companionship becomes intercession. You do not have to fix pain; you only need to stand beside it with faith. In caregiving, your nearness may speak louder than any prayer you could offer aloud. Presence is not passive; it is a living expression of grace. To sit with someone in suffering is to join them where God already is, in the space between despair and hope, and to hold that space with tenderness. Such moments remind both giver and receiver that the Lord is near and that His mercy never runs out.Jesus practiced the ministry of presence throughout His life. He lingered with the lonely, touched the unclean, and wept beside the grieving. He entered the places others avoided and turned them into sanctuaries of compassion. When you stay near to the hurting, you echo His heart. Being present becomes a form of prayer offered through body and spirit, a gift of attention that says, "You are not alone." Every time you pause to listen, sit quietly, or simply stay, you become a living reminder of Emmanuel; God with us. In your nearness, others can feel the closeness of Christ.

Reflective Questions:

Who in your life needs you to simply be present today?

How can you offer presence as prayer instead of words?

When has someone's quiet presence brought you peace?

Prayer:

Lord, thank You for being near. Let my presence reflect Your love to those who need comfort. Teach me to sit in silence with peace, to stay when others walk away, and to bring Your calm into every room I enter. Amen.

The Ministry of Presence

WEEKLY NOTES AND PRAYERS

Week 5: Faith for the Hard Days

Faith for the Hard Days

DAY 1: WHEN YOU DOUBT

Scripture:

"IMMEDIATELY THE BOY'S FATHER exclaimed, 'I do believe; help me overcome my unbelief!'" – Mark 9:24 (NIV)

Devotional Reflection:

Faith and doubt often walk side by side. You can love God deeply and still wrestle with questions about His timing, His silence, or His plan. Caregiving, especially in long seasons of fatigue or uncertainty, can magnify those doubts. You may wonder if your faith is strong enough or if your struggles somehow disappoint God. Yet Scripture reminds us that God is not threatened by honest questions. He meets His children where they are, not where they think they should be. Doubt does not disqualify you from

His grace. It can draw you deeper into dependence on Him when you bring your uncertainty into the light of prayer.

Jesus responded to the father's cry not with rebuke but with mercy. Faith is not the absence of doubt; it is the decision to trust God even when the outcome is unclear. When you whisper, "Help my unbelief," you are already reaching toward hope. Each time you face uncertainty, you have the opportunity to lean on the steadiness of Christ instead of the shifting weight of your emotions. Even fragile faith, when placed in a faithful God, becomes unshakable. The Lord delights in a heart that clings to Him through the fog, trusting that His strength will hold when yours begins to fade.

Reflective Questions:

What doubts have you been afraid to bring before God?

How has God shown grace in your moments of uncertainty?

What helps you hold on when faith feels weak?

Prayer:

Lord, thank You for welcoming my doubts with patience and grace. Strengthen my faith when I am weary and remind me that Your love never falters. Teach me to bring every question to You rather than hide in fear or shame. Let my uncertainty lead me closer to Your heart and not away from it. Help my unbelief become trust in Your steady and unchanging goodness. Amen.

Faith for the Hard Days

DAY 2: GUILT AND GRACE

Scripture:

"THEREFORE, THERE IS NOW no condemnation for those who are in Christ Jesus." – Romans 8:1 (NIV)

Devotional Reflection:

Guilt clings easily to caregivers. You question if you are doing enough, loving enough, or managing enough. The "should have" thoughts echo in your mind long after the day ends. Yet guilt is not from God; it is the voice of perfectionism trying to earn what grace has already given. Jesus carried your shortcomings to the cross so you would not have to. His grace meets you in the space between your effort and His sufficiency. You do not need to carry what He already forgave. The weight you feel is often not the burden of love but the pressure of unrealistic expectation. Grace reminds you that God never asked for perfection, only for presence and trust.

Grace invites rest where guilt demands performance. When you release self-condemnation, you make room for peace to take root. Each time you fail or falter, grace whispers, "You are still loved." The Gospel is not about flawless caregiving; it is about faithful dependence on Him. Even when your strength runs out, Christ's mercy does not. The burden of guilt breaks beneath the power of His love. Through grace, your mistakes become places where His compassion shines most clearly. You are not defined by what you cannot do but by what He has already done. In that truth, your weary soul can finally rest.

Reflective Questions:

What situations trigger guilt in your caregiving journey?

How can grace reshape the way you see your limitations?

What truth about God's forgiveness brings you peace today?

Prayer:

Father, thank You that there is no condemnation for those who belong to Christ. Teach me to release guilt and rest in Your mercy. When I feel I have fallen short, remind me that Your grace fills every gap. Replace my striving with peace and my shame with gratitude. Let my life reflect the freedom that comes from being fully forgiven and fully loved. Amen.

Faith for the Hard Days

DAY 3: ANGER AT GOD

Scripture:

"How long, Lord? Will you forget me forever? How long will you hide your face from me?" – Psalm 13:1 (NIV)

Devotional Reflection:

Few emotions feel more uncomfortable to confess than anger toward God. Yet Scripture is filled with faithful people who spoke their pain directly to Him: Job, David, Jeremiah, and even Jesus on the cross. Anger does not drive God away; it draws His compassion closer. When caregiving feels unfair or your prayers seem unanswered, frustration can harden into resentment if left unspoken. But when you bring your anger to God, you are not rebelling, you are being real with the One who already knows your heart. He does not shame you for your honesty; He welcomes it. His love is wide enough to hold both your faith and your fury.

David's laments turned to worship because he refused to hide his emotions from the Lord. He poured out his complaint and, in doing so, found comfort. Your feelings don't weaken your faith; they often reveal it at its truest. When you tell God the truth about your pain, you create space for healing to begin. Anger can become an open door to intimacy when surrendered in prayer. You may not understand why God allows certain seasons of hardship, but you can trust that He is still present within them. Faith matures not by avoiding emotion but by bringing it to the altar. Love and lament can coexist, and through both, you will find that God's grace remains steady.

Reflective Questions:

What frustrations have you been holding back from God?

How does honesty with God deepen your faith?

When have you seen God bring peace out of pain?

Prayer:

Lord, I bring You my anger, my grief, and my confusion. Thank You for receiving me with patience instead of judgment. Meet me in the tension of what I feel and what I believe. Turn my frustration into deeper faith and my sorrow into trust in Your goodness. Teach me to rest in Your unchanging love even when I do not understand. Amen.

Faith for the Hard Days

Day 4: Enduring Loss

Scripture:

"The Lord is close to the brokenhearted and saves those who are crushed in spirit." – Psalm 34:18 (NIV)

Devotional Reflection:

Loss in caregiving is not a single moment; it is a slow unfolding. You watch the person you love change, sometimes in body, sometimes in memory, sometimes in spirit, and each change brings its own kind of ache. You grieve what once was even as you keep showing up for what is. These daily losses are quiet, rarely spoken aloud, yet they cut deeply. They can wear down your joy and test your faith. God does not overlook these hidden sorrows. He sits with you in the middle of them, holding space for both your love and your lament. His comfort is not reserved for the funeral; it is present in the waiting room, the midnight hour, and the long days that feel unending. The Lord's closeness does not erase pain, but it gives you strength to face what love requires.

Jesus wept at Lazarus's tomb even though He knew resurrection was near. His tears teach us that faith does not cancel grief; it sanctifies it. In caregiving, tears are not weakness; they are love made visible. You are not called to deny your sorrow but to bring it into God's presence, where it can be tended by grace. Each time you allow yourself to mourn the losses that come along the way, you invite God's healing into places that exhaustion tries to harden. Endurance is not pretending everything is fine; it is trusting that God's mercy is deep enough for every stage of loss. He is close to the brokenhearted, even when the breaking happens little by little.

Reflective Questions:

What daily or gradual losses have you grieved in your caregiving journey?

How can you invite God's comfort into those quiet moments of sadness?

What helps you hold both love and sorrow at the same time?

Prayer:

God of mercy, meet me in the losses that others do not always see. Hold me when my heart aches for what used to be. Help me grieve without losing hope and love without growing weary. Let Your nearness steady me when change feels too heavy to bear. Teach me to find peace in Your presence, one day at a time. Amen.

Faith for the Hard Days

DAY 5: LOVING THROUGH DECLINE

Scripture:

"Love bears all things, believes all things, hopes all things, endures all things." – 1 Corinthians 13:7 (NIV)

Devotional Reflection:

Watching someone you love decline is one of the deepest trials of caregiving. It tests patience, drains strength, and breaks your heart in quiet, unseen ways. You long for the person they once were, even as you learn to love who they are now. Every loss feels personal, yet love continues to call you forward. To love through decline is to enter sacred ground, where faith becomes tangible and compassion becomes worship. This kind of love is not sentimental; it is steady, often carried out in weary hands and tearful prayers. Yet it mirrors the heart of God, who loves without retreat or regret.

Each act of care, however small, becomes an offering of love that heaven treasures and that grace sustains.

The love Paul describes in 1 Corinthians 13 is not romantic or fleeting; it is resilient and divine. It bears disappointment, believes through uncertainty, and continues to hope when the outcome does not change. This love is not fueled by emotion but by the Spirit of God working within you. When fatigue and sorrow threaten to close your heart, remember that divine love endures where human love runs out. The Lord strengthens you to keep loving even as things fade, to keep hoping even when progress feels impossible. Loving through decline is a daily resurrection, a quiet act of faith that beauty and meaning still remain in the midst of loss. You are never alone in this sacred calling; the God who is love Himself walks beside you, bearing the weight you cannot carry.

Reflective Questions:

What has been hardest about loving through decline?

Where do you see glimpses of God's love sustaining you?

How can you practice grace toward yourself in this season?

Prayer:

Lord, strengthen me to love as You love, steadily and without condition. When my heart grows weary, fill me with Your peace and patience. Remind me that every act of care matters to You. Help me love through loss with faith that endures and hope that does not fade. Let my life reflect the steadfast love that never fails. Amen.

Faith for the Hard Days

Day 6: Courage to Ask for Help

Scripture:

"CARRY EACH OTHER'S BURDENS, and in this way you will fulfill the law of Christ." – Galatians 6:2 (NIV)

Devotional Reflection:

Many caregivers quietly carry the false belief that asking for help is weakness. You tell yourself that others are too busy, or that it is your job to manage it all. But isolation is a heavy burden, and God never meant for you to bear it alone. Asking for help is not surrender; it is wisdom. It is an act of faith that recognizes both your limits and God's provision. When you allow others to share the load, you invite grace into your story. Help received is also help multiplied, because it allows others to serve as vessels of God's compassion. You were never created to do this work in solitude.

The same God who called you to love deeply also designed you to live dependently, surrounded by community and sustained by grace.

Even Jesus accepted help when He carried His cross. Simon of Cyrene stepped forward to bear part of the weight, and in doing so, shared in the mystery of redemption. The Son of God did not see help as failure but as fellowship. If He could receive it, so can you. Courage is not always loud or visible; sometimes it is the quiet honesty of admitting, "I need support." Asking for help does not diminish your strength; it deepens it. It allows the body of Christ to function as it was intended, with each person giving and receiving love in turn. You honor God not by carrying everything alone, but by allowing His strength to flow through the hands of others.

Reflective Questions:

What holds you back from asking for help?

Who could you invite into your caregiving support circle?

How can receiving help become an act of faith?

Prayer:

Father, give me courage to ask for help and humility to receive it. Surround me with people who reflect Your care and compassion. When I feel the pull to do everything alone, remind me that You never called me to carry the load by myself. Let community become a living reminder of Your faithfulness. Teach me to rest in the shared strength of Your love. Amen.

Faith for the Hard Days

DAY 7: FAITH THAT HOLDS ON

Scripture:

"LET US HOLD UNSWERVINGLY to the hope we profess, for he who promised is faithful." – Hebrews 10:23 (NIV)

Devotional Reflection:

There will be days when faith feels like holding a thread in a storm. The winds of exhaustion, grief, and fear threaten to tear it away. Yet the miracle of grace is that God never asks you to hold on alone. His hand grips yours even when your strength falters. Faith that endures is not about how tightly you can cling, but about trusting the One who refuses to let you go. When you cannot see the next step, His promise becomes your light. The same God who called you into this season has already promised to walk through it with you. He does not measure your faith by perfection but by persistence. Every breath of trust, however small, reaches His heart.

Faith matures in hardship. It shifts from emotion to conviction, from comfort to confidence. The faith that holds on through tears and trials becomes anchored in God's unchanging nature. He does not ask you to suppress fear or deny weakness; He invites you to bring them into His presence, where His strength can hold what yours cannot. Each day you choose to believe, even in the smallest way, you declare that hope still lives. The same hand that steadied Peter on the waves steadies you now. Storms may rise, but your Savior does not move. In His faithfulness, you will find the courage to keep standing.

Reflective Questions:

Where do you feel your faith being tested right now?

What truth about God's character helps you endure?

How can you remind yourself daily of His faithfulness?

Prayer:

Lord, hold me when my strength fades and my heart feels unsteady. Let my faith rest securely in Your faithfulness. Teach me to trust Your promises when I cannot see the outcome. Remind me that Your grip on me never loosens and that Your love never fails. Give me courage to keep believing that You are enough for every storm I face. Amen.

Faith for the Hard Days

WEEKLY NOTES AND PRAYERS

Week 6: Rest for the Weary

Rest for the Weary

DAY 1: RHYTHMS OF GRACE

Scripture:

"COME TO ME, ALL you who are weary and burdened, and I will give you rest." – Matthew 11:28 (NIV)

Devotional Reflection:

Caregiving easily pulls you into a constant cycle of doing. Each day demands more attention, more energy, and more sacrifice. But even Jesus withdrew from the crowds to rest. He showed that sacred rhythm matters, work and rest, serving and being still. Rest is not an interruption of ministry; it is part of it. When you rest, you acknowledge that God, not you, holds everything together. Grace teaches you to breathe again and trust that stepping back is not failure but faith.

God designed rhythm into creation itself. The sun rises and sets, the tide ebbs and flows, and your soul was made for that same pattern. True rest comes not from escaping responsibility but from releasing control. You do not earn rest; you receive it as a gift from a loving Father who wants your heart whole. Learning the rhythms of grace means discovering that rest restores more than your body; it renews your spirit and keeps love alive for the long journey ahead.

Reflective Questions:

Where are you resisting God's invitation to rest?

How might regular rest strengthen your caregiving instead of hindering it?

What would it look like to trust God with what remains undone?

Prayer:

Lord, let my care become a legacy of grace. Teach me to serve faithfully in both strength and weakness. Use my love to plant seeds that grow long after I am gone. Help me rest in Your mercy and trust You with the harvest. Amen.

Rest for the Weary

Day 2: Sabbath Mindset

Scripture:

"Then he said to them, 'The Sabbath was made for man, not man for the Sabbath.'" – Mark 2:27 (NIV)

Devotional Reflection:

The Sabbath is not merely a day off—it is a way of being. It is a rhythm of trust that says, "God is enough, even when I stop." Caregivers often struggle to embrace this truth. The needs never end, and guilt whispers that rest is neglect. Yet Jesus reminds us that rest was created for our good. Sabbath means releasing the illusion of control and allowing God to remind you that you are loved for who you are, not what you produce. True rest is not laziness; it is worship.

Practicing Sabbath begins with permission—to pause, breathe, and delight in God's presence. Even short moments of stillness can restore perspective. The heart of Sabbath is not inactivity but intimacy. When you stop striving, you discover that grace keeps working. A Sabbath mindset invites peace into the busiest days and reminds you that your worth is already secure in Christ. You are free to rest because God never stops caring for you.

Reflective Questions:

How can you begin to cultivate a Sabbath rhythm in your week?

What does rest as worship look like for you?

Where might God be inviting you to stop and simply enjoy His presence?

Prayer:

Lord, thank You for creating rest as a gift, not a rule. Help me receive Sabbath as a sign of Your love. Teach me to stop striving and to trust Your care in stillness. Amen.

Rest for the Weary

DAY 3: SAYING NO

Scripture:

"LET YOUR 'YES' BE yes, and your 'No,' no." – Matthew 5:37 (NIV)

Devotional Reflection:

The word "no" can feel uncomfortable for caregivers who want to help everyone. Yet love without limits soon becomes exhaustion without joy. Saying no is not rejection—it is stewardship. It protects your heart from depletion so you can serve from overflow rather than obligation. Boundaries are not barriers to compassion; they are expressions of wisdom. When you say no for the sake of health and peace, you are saying yes to God's design for balance.

Jesus Himself said no. He walked away from crowds to pray, refused premature demands, and trusted the Father's timing. His ministry thrived not because He did everything, but because He did the right things. You are called to the same discernment. Saying no creates space for what matters most. It allows rest to grow, relationships to breathe, and grace to flow freely again. A peaceful no can be one of the most faithful things you ever say.

Reflective Questions:

What do you need to say no to this week to protect your peace?

How does saying no create room for what God values most?

Where might guilt be keeping you from healthy boundaries?

Prayer:

Father, give me courage to say no when I must. Help me trust that setting limits honors You. Let my choices reflect wisdom, peace, and love grounded in grace. Amen.

Rest for the Weary

DAY 4: SHARED REST

Scripture:

"TWO ARE BETTER THAN one, because they have a good return for their labor: If either of them falls down, one can help the other up." – Ecclesiastes 4:9–10 (NIV)

Devotional Reflection:

Rest grows deeper in community. Isolation breeds exhaustion, but shared rest multiplies renewal. You were never meant to carry burdens alone. When you allow others into your rhythm, their presence becomes part of your healing. Rest is not selfish; it is contagious. As you rest together—through laughter, prayer, or quiet companionship—you remind one another that peace is possible, even in seasons of strain.

Jesus surrounded Himself with friends who shared life, meals, and moments of rest. Even in His heaviest hours, He longed for their nearness. Shared rest mirrors divine fellowship—the Father, Son, and Spirit in eternal communion. When you rest with others, you live out that sacred pattern. Community rest says, "We belong, we are held, and we are safe." It transforms loneliness into belonging and weariness into shared strength.

Reflective Questions:

Who in your life helps you rest well?

How can you invite others into restful connection this week?

What small way could you share peace with someone else today?

Prayer:

Lord, thank You for the gift of shared rest. Surround me with people who bring peace and remind me of Your presence. Help me find renewal in community and joy in connection. Amen.

Rest for the Weary

DAY 5: BODY AND SOUL ALIGNMENT

Scripture:

"Do you not know that your bodies are temples of the Holy Spirit, who is in you...? Therefore honor God with your bodies." – 1 Corinthians 6:19–20 (NIV)

Devotional Reflection:

Your body and soul are not separate realms—they speak to one another. Fatigue of the body can drain the spirit; peace of the spirit can restore the body. God designed you as an integrated whole, and caring for your body is a form of worship. Resting, eating well, stretching, or simply breathing deeply are not acts of indulgence but reverence. When you tend to your physical needs, you honor the Spirit who dwells within you.

Jesus cared for both body and soul. He fed the hungry, healed the sick, and invited His followers to rest. Holistic care means allowing grace to reach every part of your life. Listening to your body's signals is a spiritual practice. When you align body and soul, you experience deeper peace and greater endurance. The strength you need for caregiving flows not from constant effort, but from abiding in the balance God intended.

Reflective Questions:

How have you neglected your body while caring for others?

What practices might restore harmony between your body and soul?

How can rest become part of your worship this week?

Prayer:

Holy Spirit, thank You for dwelling within me. Help me honor You through rest and care for my body. Restore my strength and align my heart with Your peace. Amen.

Rest for the Weary

DAY 6: SLEEP WITHOUT GUILT

Scripture:

"IN PEACE I WILL lie down and sleep, for you alone, Lord, make me dwell in safety." – Psalm 4:8 (NIV)

Devotional Reflection:

Sleep often becomes the first casualty of caregiving. You lie awake rehearsing the day, worrying about tomorrow, or feeling guilty for resting while others suffer. Yet God grants sleep as a gift of trust. To sleep is to surrender control—to say, "You are God, and I am not." Guilt over rest is misplaced pride disguised as responsibility. You honor God when you sleep peacefully, acknowledging that He never slumbers, so you can.

Jesus slept in the storm, not because He was careless, but because He was confident in His Father's care. Sleep reminds you that the world keeps spinning without your effort. When you release your fears at night, you make space for grace to restore you. Resting without guilt is not laziness; it is faith in action. The pillow becomes an altar of surrender, where anxiety gives way to peace.

Reflective Questions:

What keeps you from sleeping peacefully?

How might you release control to God before bedtime?

What habits could help you receive rest as grace?

Prayer:

Lord, thank You for the gift of sleep. Quiet my anxious thoughts and fill my rest with peace. Remind me that You watch over me so I can rest in Your care. Amen.

Rest for the Weary

DAY 7: PEACE AS RESISTANCE

Scripture:

"THE LORD WILL FIGHT for you; you need only to be still." – Exodus 14:14 (NIV)

Devotional Reflection:

In a restless world, peace is a form of resistance. It refuses to let fear dictate the pace of your heart. Choosing calm when chaos demands panic is a declaration of faith. Caregivers often live in constant motion, but peace calls you to slow down and trust the unseen work of God. Stillness is not surrender to weakness—it is alignment with divine strength. Peace pushes back against the lie that you must do everything yourself.

Jesus calmed storms with a word and carried serenity wherever He went. His peace was not fragile; it was fierce. When you practice peace, you carry that same quiet authority into your world. Choosing peace amid pressure transforms how you serve, speak, and see. It becomes both shield and testimony, reminding others that grace still governs every storm. Peace is not the absence of trouble; it is the presence of Christ.

Reflective Questions:

What does it mean for you to practice peace in a hurried world?

Where might God be inviting you to slow down and trust Him more deeply?

How can peace become your daily act of faith?

Prayer:

Prince of Peace, teach me to rest in Your strength when the world feels chaotic. Let Your calm rule my heart and flow through my words and actions. Make my peace a reflection of Your presence. Amen.

Rest for the Weary

WEEKLY NOTES AND PRAYERS

Week 7: Living from Overflow

Living from Overflow

DAY 1: GRATITUDE OVERFLOW

Scripture:

"MY CUP OVERFLOWS. SURELY your goodness and love will follow me all the days of my life." – Psalm 23:5–6 (NIV)

Devotional Reflection:

Gratitude transforms the ordinary into abundance. When your heart remembers God's goodness, joy begins to spill over the edges of exhaustion. Caregiving can shrink your world to tasks and timelines, but gratitude expands it again. It shifts your focus from what is missing to what is still miraculous: the smile that returns, the shared meal, the moment of laughter. Gratitude does not ignore hardship; it sees grace shining through it. It becomes a quiet discipline of the heart, reframing your day and renewing your strength. When you pause to thank God, you invite His peace to fill the space where worry once lived and discover that even in weariness, His presence sustains you.

David sang of a cup that overflows, not because life was easy, but because God filled every empty space with His goodness. Gratitude opens your eyes to see that grace is always greater than need. The more you notice God's fingerprints in your story, the more joy grows. Gratitude turns survival into sacred endurance and transforms duty into devotion. It is the overflow of a heart that remembers who God is and lives from fullness rather than fear. When you choose to give thanks, even for small mercies, you align your heart with heaven's rhythm and find rest in the assurance that God's love will follow you all your days.

Reflective Questions:

What blessings have you overlooked in your daily routine?

How does gratitude renew your strength for caregiving?

Where do you see God's goodness overflowing in your life?

Prayer:

Lord, fill my heart with gratitude until it overflows. Teach me to see Your goodness even in difficult days. Let thanksgiving renew my joy and shift my focus from burden to blessing. Remind me that every breath is grace and every moment a gift from You. May my life overflow with praise that glorifies Your name. Amen.

Living from Overflow

DAY 2: SERVING BEYOND DUTY

Scripture:

"WHATEVER YOU DO, WORK at it with all your heart, as working for the Lord, not for human masters." – Colossians 3:23 (NIV)

Devotional Reflection:

At first, caregiving can feel like duty, a list of tasks to complete and expectations to meet. But when love begins to shape each act of care, duty becomes devotion. Serving beyond obligation means pouring grace into the smallest moments, the ones no one else sees. It means finding meaning not in applause but in obedience. When your hands grow tired and your patience wears thin, remember that every act of love offered in faith is seen by God. When you serve from the heart, caregiving becomes an act of worship, a daily offering of love to the One who first loved you. Every small gesture, every quiet act of compassion, becomes a reflection of His heart at work within you.

Jesus washed His disciples' feet not out of obligation but out of love. His service was not about position but compassion. That same Spirit moves through you when you serve without resentment or expectation. When you release the need for recognition, you make space for joy to return. Love transforms the ordinary into the holy, and every unseen act of care carries eternal weight when it is offered from overflow, not exhaustion. Serving beyond duty means allowing God's love to continue flowing through you, even when your own strength fades. In those moments, you reflect the heart of Christ, who served to the very end, not because He had to, but because love compelled Him to.

Reflective Questions:

When has your care shifted from duty to love?

How can you serve from overflow rather than obligation?

What helps you remember that your service honors God?

Prayer:

Lord, teach me to serve with joy and humility. Let every act of care reflect Your compassion and kindness. Free me from resentment and fill me with the peace that comes from serving You. When I grow weary, renew my heart with love that flows from Your Spirit. May my service bring honor to Your name and blessing to others. Amen.

Living from Overflow

DAY 3: REDEEMING THE JOURNEY

Scripture:

"AND WE KNOW THAT in all things God works for the good of those who love him." – Romans 8:28 (NIV)

Devotional Reflection:

Looking back, you can see that some of the hardest moments have shaped the deepest growth. God wastes nothing, not even your weariness. The tears, the waiting, the setbacks, and the unseen labor are all part of a redemptive story. Every hardship has carved compassion into your heart and created space for grace to dwell. The caregiving journey may not be what you expected, but in God's hands, even pain becomes purpose. He redeems what feels lost and restores what feels empty. The places that once felt barren can bloom again under the care of His mercy.

Joseph looked back on years of betrayal and suffering and saw God's hand in every step, and the same is true for you. Redemption is not about rewriting your story but seeing it through new eyes. God's goodness has been present even in the chapters that broke your heart. When you begin to trust that His grace covers every part of the journey, peace takes root. You start to see that nothing was wasted, even the waiting was holy. The road that once felt like survival becomes a testimony of endurance and hope, a living witness that God brings beauty from ashes and purpose from pain.

Reflective Questions:

What part of your journey feels difficult to see as redeemable

How might God be using your story to bring hope to others?

What blessings have emerged from places of struggle?

Prayer:

Lord, thank You for redeeming every part of my journey. Help me trust Your hand in both the pain and the progress. Let peace replace regret as I see how You have worked through all things. Give me eyes to notice Your mercy where I once saw only loss. May my story reflect the beauty of Your redemption. Amen.

Living from Overflow

DAY 4: PASSING THE BATON

Scripture:

"THEREFORE ENCOURAGE ONE ANOTHER and build each other up." – 1 Thessalonians 5:11 (NIV)

Devotional Reflection:

There comes a time in every caregiver's journey when you must hand over the baton, whether to another person, to God in surrender, or to a new season of rest. Letting go is not giving up; it is trusting that the One who called you to serve will continue His work through others. You have carried much with grace, and now God invites you to release what is no longer yours to hold. Passing the baton requires courage because it means loosening your grip on what has become familiar. Yet it is also an act of love. The same God who strengthened you will sustain those who come after you. Letting go is not failure; it is faith in motion, a declaration that God's care reaches farther than your hands can stretch.

Moses watched Joshua lead the people into the Promised Land, knowing his part of the journey was complete. His legacy was obedience, not control. When you release with gratitude instead of regret, you make room for renewal. Someone else will carry the work forward, but your faith becomes part of the foundation they stand on. Passing the baton is not the end of your ministry; it is the sacred continuation of God's faithfulness through every generation. Your caregiving becomes a thread in a much larger story of grace. The same God who began the work through you will be faithful to complete it.

Reflective Questions:

What are you being called to release to God today?

Who might God be preparing to carry forward what you began?

How can letting go become an act of trust instead of fear?

Prayer:

Lord, teach me to release with grace and confidence in Your plan. Help me trust that Your work continues even when my part is done. Let my obedience bear fruit in those who follow after me. When I let go, fill me with peace instead of regret. May my faith leave behind a legacy that glorifies You. Amen.

Living from Overflow

Day 5: Legacy of Care

Scripture:

"HIS MERCY EXTENDS TO those who fear him, from generation to generation." – Luke 1:50 (NIV)

Devotional Reflection:

Your faithfulness leaves an imprint that reaches farther than you can see. Every quiet prayer, every act of kindness, every late-night vigil becomes part of a legacy that continues long after the season of caregiving ends. Legacy is not formed by grand gestures but by small, steady offerings of love given over time. When you serve with grace, you plant seeds that will outlive your strength. Others will learn compassion by watching you endure with hope.

Your consistency speaks louder than words, showing that love anchored in God's mercy can weather any storm. The work of your hands and the tenderness of your heart are threads in a tapestry that God is still weaving. What feels ordinary now will one day be recognized as sacred.

Mary's song reminds us that God's mercy echoes through generations. The care you give now will ripple into lives you may never meet. Every moment of patience, every whispered prayer, every act of forgiveness writes God's story into the hearts around you. When you love without expecting recognition, you mirror the enduring compassion of Christ. Even in exhaustion, your faith tells others what hope looks like in real time. One day, someone will draw strength from your example, remembering that grace was stronger than weariness. Your legacy of care is not about what you accomplish, but about who you have become in the process—a living reflection of mercy that will keep speaking long after your work is done.

Reflective Questions

Who has left a legacy of grace in your life?

How might your care impact others for years to come?

What small act today could plant a seed of lasting love?

Prayer:

Father, thank You that nothing given in love is ever wasted. Let my care reflect Your mercy and endure beyond my own strength. Use my faithfulness to inspire hope in those who follow after me. Teach me to love in ways that plant seeds of grace for generations to come. May my legacy always point others to Your goodness. Amen.

Living from Overflow

Day 6: Joy Rekindled

Scripture:

"Restore to me the joy of your salvation and grant me a willing spirit, to sustain me." – Psalm 51:12 (NIV)

Devotional Reflection:

Over time, caregiving can dim the light of joy. The weight of responsibility, constant decisions, and steady fatigue can press your spirit flat. Yet joy is not fragile, and it is never truly lost. It waits patiently beneath the layers of duty, ready to rise again. Joy rekindled is not about pretending everything is fine but about remembering that God's presence is greater than your burden. Even in the quiet, ordinary moments, He is near, and His nearness can still spark gladness. When you pause long enough to notice beauty, a kind word, a moment of laughter, a glimpse of grace, you begin to remember that joy was never gone, only hidden under the noise of survival.

David prayed for joy to be restored, not replaced, because joy was always meant to return. God delights in reviving what feels weary and breathing life into hearts that have forgotten how to smile. Joy is not the absence of hardship but the evidence of hope. It bubbles up through tears, whispers through weariness, and testifies that grace still reigns. When you welcome joy back into your day, you bear witness to a God who restores what the world cannot replace. Joy becomes the overflow of gratitude and trust, the quiet proof that God's love still fills every broken space with light.

Reflective Questions:

What moments have recently sparked joy in your heart?

How might joy become a daily spiritual practice again?

Where has God brought new life where you once felt empty?

Prayer:

Lord, rekindle my joy and renew my strength. Let Your presence lift the heaviness that settles over my heart. Teach me to find delight again in simple moments of grace. Restore the laughter that reminds me You are near. Help me live from the overflow of Your joy today. Amen.

Living from Overflow

DAY 7: PRAYER OF RELEASE

Scripture:

"CAST ALL YOUR ANXIETY on him because he cares for you." – 1 Peter 5:7 (NIV)

Devotional Reflection:

Release is not giving up; it is giving over. After days and nights of caregiving, you may find your heart heavy with what cannot be fixed or changed. God invites you to lay down what was never meant to rest solely in your hands. Surrender is not weakness; it is faith in action. When you release your fear, your exhaustion, and your sorrow into His care, you make room for peace to settle where striving once lived. Letting go is a sacred exchange—your burdens for His rest, your anxiety for His assurance. The act of release allows you to breathe again, to remember that you are held by the One who never tires, never falters, and never lets go.Jesus' final words on the cross were a prayer of release: "Father, into Your hands I commit my spirit." His surrender was not the end of His story; it was the doorway to resurrection. The same invitation stands before you. As you open your hands, what feels like loss becomes the soil for renewal. You are not stepping away from purpose; you are stepping deeper into presence. When you entrust your cares to God, He does what only He can—He restores what was broken and strengthens what was fragile. In His hands, even your surrender becomes an act of worship.

Reflective Questions:

What burdens are you ready to release into God's care?

How can surrender bring you freedom instead of fear?

Where do you sense God inviting you to rest in His hands?

Prayer:

Father, I release what I cannot carry into Your perfect care. Quiet my heart where fear has settled and fill me with peace. Teach me to trust You with what I cannot control. Help me rest in the safety of Your presence and breathe deeply of Your grace. Let surrender become my song of faith and freedom. Amen.

Living from Overflow

WEEKLY NOTES AND PRAYERS

About the Author

DWANE J. BROWN

DWANE IS a husband, caregiver, musician, ordained chaplain, and lifelong student of God's Word. He holds an MBA and is pursuing advanced studies in theology with a focus on pastoral care and spiritual formation. Over the years, he has served in worship ministry, men's ministry, prayer ministry, community care ministry, Kairos Prison Ministry, and Walk to E mmaus.

Before becoming an author, Dwane spent decades in leadership and mentoring roles, helping people grow through seasons of challenge and change. Those same gifts now shape his writing, where he blends practical encouragement with grace-centered hope.

Most importantly, he writes this series as a caregiver himself, serving his wife, the love of his life and his first ministry. His heart is to encourage caregivers to see their journey not only as service but as sacred ground where God's grace meets daily life.

Connect with Dwane

Website: www.GraceFilledPress.com

Email: chaplaindwane@gmail.com

Facebook: facebook.com/dwanejbrown

Instagram: @ChaplainDwane

If this devotional encouraged you, please consider leaving an honest review on Amazon or Goodreads. Reviews help other caregivers discover the support they need.

www.ingramcontent.com/pod-product-compliance
Lightning Source LLC
La Vergne TN
LVHW051414080426
835508LV00022B/3079